R. N Boyd

Petroleum

its development and uses

R. N Boyd

Petroleum
its development and uses

ISBN/EAN: 9783337414238

Printed in Europe, USA, Canada, Australia, Japan

Cover: Foto ©Andreas Hilbeck / pixelio.de

More available books at **www.hansebooks.com**

ITS DEVELOPMENT AND USES

BY

R. NELSON BOYD

MEMBER OF THE INSTITUTION OF CIVIL ENGINEERS

WHITTAKER AND CO.,

2, WHITE HART STREET, PATERNOSTER SQUARE, LONDON,

AND 66, FOURTH AVENUE, NEW YORK.

1895.

PREFACE

THE enormous and increasing consumption of petroleum of various qualities in this country has created a special interest in this useful natural product, and the author has met with frequent inquiries from users of oil outside the trade as to its origin, manner of production, and mode of preparation. The following pages have been written with a view to giving some general information on the subject. It has not been attempted to compile a text-book, but simply to collect a few facts about petroleum which may prove of interest to the reader.

Mr. A. H. Rowan, A.M.I.C.E., has kindly written a special chapter on "Petroleum Engines," which will be found useful and interesting.

R. N. B.

London, February 1895.

CONTENTS

APPENDICES.

PETROLEUM

CHAPTER I

INTRODUCTORY

SINCE the introduction of petroleum into this country the consumption has continuously and enormously increased. In 1859 the imports into the United Kingdom amounted to 2,000,000, and in 1893 they had reached a total of 155,126,667 gallons. The Board of Trade returns do not specify the various kinds of oil which are included in the above figures. As a matter of fact, very little crude petroleum, if any, is imported into the United Kingdom. By far the largest proportion consists of illuminating oil, termed "petroleum oil" by the trade in Great Britain, and "kerosene" in the United States. A certain quantity of petroleum spirit or gasoline, and lubricating oils, and so-called solar oil for the enrichment of gas, are included in the above figures, leaving probably in round numbers 130,000,000 gallons of oil consumed for lighting and heating purposes, and also for the production of power in the motors known as petroleum engines. To the quantity of petroleum imported must be added the mineral oil

B

produced in Scotland from the 2,000,000 tons of shale raised and treated, which will probably amount to 20,000,000 gallons of illuminating oil.

The large amount of petroleum oil now used for purposes other than lighting may be roughly computed by comparing the quantity imported ten years ago, when the petroleum stove and motor were almost unknown, with that recorded for 1893. We find that in 1883 the imports of petroleum oil amounted to 50,000,000 gallons, and in 1893 to about 155,000,000 gallons. It is hardly necessary to point out the numerous advantages to be derived from a regular supply of this useful product. For illuminating purposes, more especially in the smaller houses, it stands without a rival; and in recent years the oil-stove has come into very general use, more particularly in households where gas is not laid on. The petroleum-oil engine is now applied to many purposes in place of the steam-engine or the gas-engine. One great advantage possessed by these motors lies in the fact that an oil-engine can be applied in any situation where a cask or a ten-gallon jar of oil can be delivered. The oil-engine may prove of great advantage to the gold-mines in Western Australia, where water is scarce, and is already in use at some mines.

The transport and storage of such a large quantity of inflammable oil are matters requiring the most careful consideration, with a view to safety. At the wharves and stores in London the stocks sometimes amount to over 20,000,000 gallons, and at a single wharf as much as 4,000,000 gallons have been stored at one time. As the law stands at present, no regulations exist as to quantities stored or the manner of effecting such storage for petroleum having a flashing point 73° F. close test. Yet it is obvious that certain precautions are necessary to prevent accidents in handling enormous quantities of inflammable liquid; and in view of opinions expressed by authorities in these matters, a Select Committee of the House of Commons was appointed last session to inquire into the subject of petroleum. This Committee has met on several occasions, and collected some evidence before adjourning until this session, when it will probably be re-appointed.

Considering the large quantity of petroleum consumed in the United Kingdom for various purposes, and its great value as a source of light and heat to the millions who have to study economy, it is presumed that a few pages on such a subject may prove acceptable to the reading public.

CHAPTER II

ALTHOUGH the general use of petroleum as an illuminant, lubricant, heat and power producer, etc., dates from a comparatively recent period, it has been known, and to some extent used, from times of the greatest antiquity. There are numerous references in the Bible to pitch and slime, which must refer to some variety of bitumen, and as mention is also made of liquid pitch and burning gas, it is not unreasonable to conclude that the pitch of the Bible may have been nothing else than petroleum exudations dried by the heat of the sun. We are told, among other allusions to the substance, that Noah's ark was pitched "within and without," and that in the construction of the Tower of Babel "slime had they for mortar," which in all probability was petroleum dried by the heat of the sun. Asphalt or pitch was known to the ancient Egyptians, who used it for embalming their dead, and also for pavements, as the latter have been found among Assyrian ruins. These very ancient records do not directly allude to the application of liquid pitch, although its use either for lighting or other purposes may have been known to people in remote antiquity.

One of the very early applications of petroleum was undoubtedly as a medicine, and it is mentioned as such by Arabian writers as far back as 370 B.C. Without tracing minutely the historical references to petroleum, I may mention that Posidonius refers to the dark oil used in lamps, and in the Talmud the burning of white naphtha is forbidden on the Sabbath, on account of the danger of fire. Pliny, in writing about naphtha and its uses, refers to it as a lubricant, and Strabo records the presence of asphaltum in the Dead Sea, anciently called " Asphaltites Lacus." The first allusion to the existence of petroleum in Europe is probably made by Herodotus, who minutely describes the occurrence of petroleum springs in the island of Zante. Different Latin authors frequently allude to the petroleum of Sicily found near the present town of Girgenti. The first records during the Christian era are by Mossadi, who died A.D. 950, and Marco Polo, who visited Baku in the latter part of the thirteenth century. The burning petroleum jets of the peninsula of Apsheron were undoubtedly the object of adoration by the degenerate followers of the religion of Zoroaster, and the remains of the temples erected for the purpose of fire-worship may be traced at the present time. These temples have been proved to have a strong resemblance to those of the Punjaub, admittedly constructed for the use of fire-worshippers. It is singular to have to record that of all the points mentioned by ancient writers as yielding naphtha or petroleum, the great South Russian field is the only one where it is raised in quantity at the present time, excepting perhaps China and Burmah.

Apsheron has had many rulers. Originally it belonged
to Persia, then the Emperor Heraclius captured it A.D.
620—627, and destroyed the temples of the fire-worshippers. Afterwards it fell into the hands of the Arabs.
It subsequently reverted to Persia, and in the middle
ages the raising of petroleum at Baku formed a monopoly
of the Persian monarch, who derived a considerable
income from persons who farmed the mines. It appears
to have been principally used for lighting purposes, as
Marco Polo says that people came from a great distance,
even from Bagdad, to purchase oil to burn. The working
of these mines seems to have been continuous, for in
1728, when Peter the Great conquered Baku, he found a
flourishing trade in existence, which had to be regulated.
The Persians recovered Baku after the death of Peter the
Great, and held it until 1806, when it was definitely
occupied by Russia. The working of petroleum was then
declared a monopoly and leased, and in the year 1850
the income derived from this source amounted to 80,000
roubles (about £7000). The Government tax at that time
was 35 kopeks, say 8*d.* per pood of 36 lbs., equal to about
6*s.* per barrel of 42 gallons. It is worthy of notice that
this development of the trade in Russia took place before
the discovery of kerosene or lamp-oil by distillation. The
crude oil was burnt in open earthenware lamps, and was
also used as fuel. The manner of raising the petroleum is
described as follows by Rossmasler in 1860—"The naphtha
was raised by hand or horse-power, according to the depth
and yield of the well, in buckets made of goatskin, with
an iron ring fixed on the open end. It was then carried

by means of open channels to underground tanks with flat roofs, and from these it was delivered to the purchasers, who filled their so-called burdgugi, and loaded them on camels or arbens, which are small wooden carts with wheels six or seven feet in height. A burdgugi is made of the entire skin of a goat or ox." The introduction of boring in the Baku district dates from the year 1860.

The first attempts at distillation were made in Russia in 1850, but with pitch, not oil; it was not until 1860 that the crude oil was distilled. The Russian trade increased rapidly, more especially after the trade had been declared free by ukase dated February 17, 1872.

Although Baku is the oil-field most largely developed in Europe, it is not the only district where petroleum has been known to exist for centuries.

In Bavaria it was known in 1430, and raised and sold by monks under the name of "oil of St. Quirinius" for medicinal purposes.

In Hanover it was known and used in the sixteenth century. Agricola, writing in 1546, refers to liquid bitumen in the neighbourhood of Brunswick. The district of Oelheim, in Hanover, where oil has been known to exist for many years, extends some forty miles in length, the surface of which is covered with drift sand, into which the oil at certain points filtrates, forming pit-holes of oil, which has been used in the neighbour-hood as a lubricator for cart-wheels, and also as a medi-cine. In 1769 the oil was described by a professor of that day, who stated that it contained 60 per cent. of petroleum and some naphtha. Over twenty years ago the

Hanoverian Government caused bore-holes to be sunk in the vicinity of Celle and Peine to depths of fifty to two hundred feet, which proved the existence of oil in small quantities. Several attempts have been made to develop this district in recent times by boring down to greater depths, but no large quantities of oil have been found. There is, however, a small production at the present time.

In various other places in Germany petroleum has been discovered, but the most important is Pechelbronn in Elsass. It is recorded in 1498 that bitumen had been raised in this place for years, and in 1625 a book was written on the "earth balsam, petrolei, and soft amber" of Pechelbronn, and according to this book the oil was mostly used as medicine, but also as a lubricant and illuminant. This district has in recent years been developed, and proved to be highly productive.

In France it is known to exist, and the deposit of Gabian in Herault was noted in 1752.

In Italy it was known to the ancients at Girgenti, and the oil in Lombardy, near Parma and Modena, was described by François Ariosto in 1660, and it is raised in small quantities at the present time, in those districts.

In Galicia, Austria, the oil industry is of ancient standing, and as elsewhere oil was first used as medicine. It is mentioned by an author writing in 1506 as "earth balsam," but it was also used as cart-wheel grease, and exported to Russia for the purpose of rendering leather water-tight. From this date on, there are numerous references to the working of petroleum and earth wax or ozocerite in Galicia, and the manufacture of candles is recorded in

Drohobycz in 1817. It is even stated that about that time, at the above-named place, an attempt was made to distil the crude and produce a refined illuminating oil. Certain it is that the Burgomaster of Prague referred to the new illuminant in 1817 for street lighting, and ordered 300 cwts., at a cost of thirty-four florins, to be delivered. The oil, however, was delayed in transit, and consequently the practical distillation of petroleum was postponed for years in Galicia. It was not until 1853 or 1854 that a Jew named Schreiner, while heating crude oil in order to produce an improved lubricant, observed a white liquid which had condensed on the cover of the vessel containing the oil, and took the substance to an apothecary in Lemberg, who discovered its value for lighting purposes, and at once constructed a still and began perhaps for the first time to manufacture illuminating petroleum oil. From that time on, the oil industry in Galicia developed, but on a comparatively small scale, until the modern improvements from the United States were introduced some few years ago.

In North America the existence and value of petroleum had been known to the aborigines, who used it for medicinal purposes, and gathered it by spreading their blankets over streams in the vicinity of outcrops, where the oil was seen floating on the surface of the water. The first notice of petroleum in North America is contained in a letter from a monk named d'Allion, written in 1629. General Montcalm in 1755 mentions that the Seneca Indians were in the habit of setting fire to the oil floating on the surface of the river

Alleghany during religious ceremonies. Towards the end of the eighteenth century it was sold as Seneca oil for the cure of rheumatism, at the rate of one dollar a gallon. In those days the oil was collected either by spreading thick woollen blankets on the streams carrying oil floating on the surface of the water and then wringing them, or it was skimmed with big spoons out of small shallow pits. The production was self-evidently very small. It was in boring for salt brine that the existence of larger quantities of petroleum underground was discovered. In the year 1806 boring for brine was first introduced in West Virginia, and this method of winning brine became generally adopted. Many of these bore-holes yielded petroleum as well as brine, so much so that it is recorded that in 1856 from fifty to one hundred barrels of oil were collected yearly. But the petroleum was looked on in those days as an impurity and dreaded by the salters.

CHAPTER III

HAVING briefly glanced at the historical records connected with petroleum, I shall now consider the discoveries
which have led to the present enormous production, and
the creation of the great industry connected with the
treatment of the crude oil. It is a curious fact that in
the main the uses to which petroleum is at present
applied are practically the same now as they were many
years ago; only formerly the oil was applied in primi-
tive appliances and rude fashion, whereas at present we
have the benefit of the numerous improvements and
inventions founded on experience and created by science.
The Persians used crude oil for lighting purposes
in open lamps as well as for fuel, the monks of the
middle ages applied it as a medicine, and the farmers of
Germany found it useful as a grease for their cart-wheels.
At the present day it is distilled and subdivided into
kerosene or burning oil, one of the most widely-distributed
illuminants, into heavy or lubricating oils, and lastly
into solid hydrocarburets, such as paraffin, which is used
for making candles and vaseline, and other pharma-
ceutical products used in medicines. Of course we now
have applications suited to modern inventions which

could not have been thought of in olden times, for example, the petroleum-oil engine and the gas enrichment process.

Science and practical invention are extending the useful application of the products obtained by fractional distillation of the crude oil, and from day to day new products are discovered and extracted from the decomposed crude oil, now that the quantity produced is so abundant. The great hindrance to the introduction of petroleum for practical application, for years after its great value was known, was the limited amount raised. The first step towards an increased production was the bore-hole sunk in 1859 near Titusville, in the United States. Long before that date, the value of petroleum oil as an illuminant and lubricator had been ascertained in Europe and the United States, but owing to the small quantity produced it had not entered the markets as an article of commerce. As a matter of fact the shale and coal oils were the precursors of petroleum. The manufacture of illuminating oil from coal or shale dates back to 1840, when such oils were produced in France. Subsequently, a large trade in shale oil was established in Scotland. In Galicia the development of the petroleum-fields was stimulated by a desire to replace the costly coal oil used on the Northern Railway of Austria, and in the United States shale oil was extensively used under the name of rock oil or kerosene.

In 1853 the first attempt was made in the United States to manufacture kerosene from petroleum; and Mr. G. Bissel founded the Pennsylvania Rock Oil Company for that purpose, and proceeded to open out an oil property near Titusville, by digging wells and trenches. The undertaking was not successful, owing to the small quantity of oil which was obtained from the shallow wells, and the only result of the company's operations was an exhaustive analysis and report by Professor B. Siliman, jun., on the oil.

Professor Siliman applied fractional distillation, and used sulphuric acid for purification, a proceeding which continues to be in use at refineries to this day. He pointed out the valuable products to be obtained by distillation, and foreshadowed in this important report the possibilities to be realized by a correct method of treating petroleum. It was not, however, until some years later that Mr. G. Bissel had the happy idea of tapping the subterranean stores of crude oil by means of deep bore-holes, and Mr. E. L. Drake, who had for some time given his attention to the subject, was entrusted with the duty of carrying out the scheme, and he put down a bore-hole near Titusville which on August 28, 1859, struck oil at a depth ·of 169½ feet, which gave about 25 barrels per day. This date is an epoch in the history of the petroleum industry, which may indeed be considered to have come into practical existence on that day. The tapping of oil in the celebrated Drake well acted like an electric spark on the spirit of American speculators, and they made a frantic rush for the oil-fields which can only be compared to the gold-craze of California. Well after well was sunk, and soon flowing wells were struck, which poured out oil at the rate of several thousand barrels per day. This naturally increased the fever of speculation.

Every farm within miles of an oil-well was bought up, and the stillness of the forests soon became broken by the jingle of the machinery and the thud of the chisel from the numerous rigs at work. Towns rose up into existence apparently from the soil, not in years or months, but in days—wherever oil was discovered, and disappeared as rapidly from the surface on the subsidence of the flow. I will cite Pithole City as an example of this ephemeral existence: a town which in May 1865 contained ten houses, when the celebrated well "United States" struck oil, and in August of the same year, that is to say about one hundred days later, it contained a population of 14,000 people, and was the centre of a daily production of 5000 barrels of oil. But the wells soon gave out, and within one year the bustling population had migrated to better ground, and left nothing but a few decaying wooden houses, which were burnt to the ground by a fire, and all that remained to mark the spot where the once busy town stood was a heap of ashes. This is by no means a singular instance, as hundreds of villages, towns, and cities were brought into existence in haste by the magic-like power of the dollar-flowing oil, and abandoned with equal alacrity when the stream began to slacken. Not only towns sprang into sudden life in formerly desolate spots, but whole districts were covered with derricks, and the ground was perforated by innumerable wells in an amazingly short space of time, to be soon deserted and once more left to the farmer or lumber-man. The intense speculation of the day created an irrational development, and wells were sunk all over immense tracts with little or no prospect of success, but on the chance not so much of striking oil as of striking an over-sanguine purchaser, and this was termed "wild-catting." This sort of swindle was carried on to such an extent by the army of so-called mystery men, scouts, and others, that at a meeting of oilmen held at Bradford on September 30, 1884, the following resolution was passed—"Resolved, that the practice of barricading and guarding derricks with bull-dogs and firearms ought not to be tolerated in a civilized community." This resolution gives an insight into the condition of the oil districts in the early days of discovery.

Meanwhile, the development of the industry was progressing in the hands of more serious workers, and some idea can be formed of its rapid growth by the returns of oil raised. In the early years these were not accurate, as a great deal of the oil was wasted owing to insufficient tankage, and millions of barrels of oil may be estimated to have been lost at the commencement of well-drilling. Yet the figures speak eloquently to the rapidity of the increase of production. In 1859, the year of the first bore-hole or well, the production is returned at 2000 barrels; two years later, that is in 1861, it had increased to 2,110,000, or one hundredfold; in 1882 it was 30,460,000 barrels. Since then the production has further increased, and in 1891 it amounted to 54,291,980, in 1892 the return was 50,509,136, and in 1893 it fell to 48,412,666 barrels of 42 American gallons.

This great development has necessitated: first, an improved system of drilling; secondly, a new mode of transport; thirdly, the creation of extensive refineries.

In drilling, the development took place after the introduction of machinery, the first engine being used at Tidiante in 1860, and the first pipe-line laid in 1863. There are many thousand miles of pipe-line of different dimensions in the United States at present.

The use of nitro-glycerine was introduced and patented by Colonel Roberts in 1866, the object being to explode a charge of nitro-glycerine at the bottom of the wells, in order to shatter the rock and thereby increase the flow of oil. The charge at first varied from 2 to 8 quarts of nitro-glycerine, but was afterwards increased up to 100 quarts. This new invention brought into existence an illicit trade for the manufacture of nitro-glycerine and the firing of wells without paying the patent Royalty, and the men who carried on this business were known as " moonlighters."

Coeval with the development of the petroleum industry in the United States, the opening out of the oil-fields of Galicia (Austria) took place. Although the apothecary at Lemberg, as previously mentioned, had erected a still and made kerosene, and had even lit up the hospital at Lemberg with it in 1855, the trade remained stationary owing to the very small production, which then was raised out of shallow shafts one metre square, by drawing the oil in buckets by hand. In Galicia, as in every oil-field, development followed improved drilling. An abortive attempt at drilling by engine-power in this field was made in 1867; but the first practical introduction of machinery was in 1882, and since then the production of crude oil has enormously increased, as the following figures show : in 1882 the production was 319,500 barrels;

in 1888 it had risen to 2,400,000 barrels, and in 1893 to about 3,000,000. In Galicia the industry is hampered by want of transport, and nine-tenths of the oil is still conveyed to the railway in barrels.

The oil-fields of the United States and of Galicia were the first to become developed. These were succeeded by the Baku field in Russia. This oil-field, although known in times of remote antiquity and continuously worked for centuries, has only recently been opened out to any extent. In 1869 the first boring operations were undertaken ; in 1872 the raising and working of oil was declared free by the Government, and from that date the development has continued with amazing rapidity. In 1873 the production was 450,000 barrels; in 1883 it had risen to $5\frac{1}{2}$ million barrels, and in 1890 over 20,000,000 barrels. The oil-fields of Southern Russia are the most productive of any known, the wells are mostly flowing, and one of them is recorded to have thrown up 112,000 tons of oil in the first four weeks following the strike of the oil.

Although petroleum is known to exist in nearly every part of the world, no great developments have as yet taken place beyond those just recorded. The best field which has been opened out to some extent and shows a promising future is that of Pechelbronn in Elsass, Germany. For many years solid bitumen has been extensively worked in this neighbourhood, but very little oil. Only within quite recent years have bore-holes been put down, with the result that at present a flourishing industry has been established.

In Canada the oil-field of Petrolia has been opened out

c

simultaneously with the American fields. But the production has never risen to any great importance, and at present the output is about 500,000 barrels.

In the far East petroleum has been worked for centuries, but only of late years has the development attained considerable proportions, notably in Japan, Java, Burmah, and some parts of India. As far as Great Britain is concerned, the supply of petroleum, including all the oils of varying densities and uses, comes from the United States and Russia only.

CHAPTER IV

THE ORIGIN OF PETROLEUM, AND GEOLOGICAL STRATA IN WHICH IT IS FOUND

WITHOUT going into scientific details, it may be interesting to record the principal hypotheses advanced to explain the presence of bitumens of all kinds in the earth. These may be divided into two classes, namely, the inorganic and the organic, the former referring to chemical changes in inorganic substances, and the latter to changes in organic matter. These hypotheses are as follows.

. Firstly, as to inorganic origin—

✓1. M. Berthelot's theory is founded on contact of carbonated waters with alkali metals.

✓2. M. Mendelejeff depends on the contact of water with highly-heated metallic iron and metallic carbides.

Secondly, as to organic origin—

1. Bischoff assumes a primary decomposition of vegetable substances contained in sedimentary strata.

2. Newbery advocates a slow decomposition at low temperatures of organic matter (mainly vegetable), such as is contained in shales.

3. Hunt's theory of origin is through the decomposition of organic matter accumulated in limestone.

4. Coquand refers to the primary decomposition of

organic matter in deep-lying strata, and accumulations in newer strata at the time of deposition through the action of springs.

5. Lartet's theory of origin is through the distillation of organic matter in deep-lying strata accompanying metamorphism by pressure and the action of superheated water.

6. Peckham believes that certain bitumens are of animal origin and indigenous in the rocks, and others of vegetable origin and the product of distillation under the influence of heat generated by organic movement.

7. Orton modifies Hunt's hypothesis, and supposes the origin to be through the primary decomposition of animal and vegetable tissue contained in shales and limestone.

The recent researches have led geologists to reject the inorganic theories and to admit the organic or animal origin of bitumens, including petroleum and all hydrocarbons, and to accept the views of Bischoff, namely, that the various bitumens are produced by the natural decomposition of organic tissue.

These different theories have been very clearly summarized in the report of the United States Geological Survey, 1886-87, as follows—

1. Petroleum is derived from organic matter.

2. It is much more largely derived from vegetable than from animal substances.

3. Petroleum of the Pennsylvania type is derived from the organic matter of bituminous shales, and is of vegetable origin.

4. Petroleum of the Canada and Lima type is derived from limestone, and is of animal origin.

5. Petroleum has been produced at normal earth temperatures (in these fields), and is not a product of destructive distillation of bituminous shales.

6. The stock of petroleum in the rocks is already practically complete.

Scientific men in Europe ascribe nearly all the petroleum and bitumen deposits of the Continent, such as those of Galicia, Germany, and Russia, to an animal origin, or a mixture of animal and small proportion of vegetable matter. The animal origin of petroleum is supported by the fact that in most bitumens a certain percentage of nitrogen is found to exist.

The fact that extensive deposits of animal fossiliferous remains are found in many geological strata without the presence of petroleum, must be explained by the supposition that the circumstances under which these animal deposits were formed were not favourable to a decomposition resulting in the production of petroleum. The recent experiments of Dr. Engler confirm the theory of the animal origin of some petroleums. He obtained what may be described as petroleum, containing almost all the hydrocarbons contained in the natural product, by distilling animal fats and oils at a moderate heat under pressure, and these experiments go far to support the theory of the origin of petroleum from the decomposition of extinct animals. It may be pointed out that oil is frequently found in strata devoid of any trace of past animal life; but it is well known that petroleum flows for long distances from the point of its production or storage in the earth, and frequently comes up to the surface at a great distance from the spot where it is tapped underground by the drill.

Whatever may be the origin of petroleum, its existence has been demonstrated in more or less quantities in nearly every stratified formation of the earth. We find it in the Post-Tertiary or Pleistocene formation in Hanover and Canada, in the Tertiary in France, Italy, Java, New Zealand, and California; in Roumania, Turkey, Galicia (Austria), Russia, Venezuela, and various localities in Asia. In the Secondary or Mesozoic it is found in Spain, Italy, Galicia (Austria), some places in Germany, Portugal, and Argentina. The Palæozoic formation yields petroleum in France, Germany, England, Pennsylvania, Ohio, and Kansas. In the Devonian and Silurian in the United States and Canada. The most important oil deposits are found either in Tertiary strata, as in Russia and Galicia (Austria), or in the Devonian, as in the United States and Canada. This universal presence of petroleum points to the great probability that it is not necessarily found in the strata where it was originally formed. There are no special geological features accompanying or indicating the presence of oil. It announces its presence by coming out of small fissures on the surface, either in the shape of liquid or gaseous carburetted hydrogen. It has been often assumed that there is some connection between petroleum and rock-salt, because the water in petroleum-fields is frequently saline. But there is no absolute proof forthcoming that the presence of salt is essential to the existence of petroleum.

CHAPTER V

PETROLEUM, as it comes out of the earth, consists of a mixture of different hydrocarbons, varying in consistency from marsh gas to solid paraffin wax, in density from 0·550 to 0·980, and in the relative proportions of hydrogen to carbon from 1 to 3 up to 1 to 5½. There are two well-defined series of hydrocarbons to be found in petroleum; first, the paraffin series, represented by the chemical formula $CnH_2n + 2$, and the olefin series, having for typical formula CnH_2n. By far the greater proportion of the hydrocarbons in all petroleums belong to the former series, and in some mineral oils the latter series are entirely missing; as a rule they are found in oils of high density, such as the Russian. In addition to the hydrocarbons, petroleum generally contains small proportions of other substances, such as oxygen, nitrogen, sulphur, and occasionally small quantities of mineral bodies such as arsenic, lime, oxide of iron, alumina, and even gold and silver.

The following table, showing the composition of some

crude oils, is taken from Professor Hans Hofer's book on petroleum.

LOCALITY.	CARBON.	HYDROGEN.	OXYGEN.	DENSITY.
Galicia....................	85·3	12·6	2·1	0·855
Elsass	86·1	12·7	1·2	0·892
Parma	84·0	13·4	1·8	0·790
Baku	83·3	11·6	3·1	0·954
Burmah	83·8	12·7	3·5	0·875
Java	87·1	12·0	0·9	0·923
Canada....................	84·5	13·5	2·0	0 870
Pennsylvania	82·0	14·8	3·2	0·730
Do.	84·9	13·7	1·4	0·880

According to Crew, the American oil is assumed to contain, on the average, 84 per cent. of carbon and 14 per cent. of hydrogen.

The treatment of natural petroleum in order to separate it into commercial products consists in distilling the crude oil in retorts of suitable construction, and condensing the products passing over at different temperatures. Thus, roughly speaking, the products may be divided into three groups : first, the volatile oils passing over at temperatures up to 150° C.; second, the illuminating oils from 150° to 300° C.; and thirdly, the residuum. The distillation is a destructive one, and the condensed oils are not in the same molecular condition as the crude oils coming out of the earth. The distillation is, however, carried on fractionally, so that a large number of products are obtained, thus—

I. *Distillates below* 150° *C.*

Rhigolene, gasolene, naphtha, benzine, ligroine, etc.

II. *Distillates from* 150° *to* 300° *C.*

Various qualities of lamp-oil or kerosene.

III. *Residuum, distillates over* 300° *C.*

Various heavy oils, such as the Russian solar distillate, and a series of lubricating oils; then paraffin oils out of which paraffin wax is made, and very dense, pitch-like oils used as fuel. The distillation leaves a residue of coke.

The proportions of the substances obtained from different oils vary considerably. Peckham gives the following results for Pennsylvanian oil—

Volatile oils	16·5
Kerosene	54·0
Lubricating oils	17·5
Paraffin	2·0
Coke and loss	10·0
	100·0

According to Ludwig Nobel, the Baku oil contains—

Volatile oils	4·0
Kerosene	27·0
Lubricating oils	44·0
Vaseline	1·0
Residuum or astatki	14·0
Loss	10·0
	100·0

Youngs' mineral oil, according to Mr. Boverton Redwood—

Volatile oils	6·0
Illuminating oils	38·0
Lubricating oils	14·5
Solid paraffin	11·0
Loss	30·5
	100·0

It will be seen from these analyses that the volatile oils are present in much larger quantities in the American than in the Russian or Scotch shale oil.

The products obtained in the refining process of petroleum have every one a value, and the various distillates are all applicable to different uses. The volatile oils for surgical purposes, street naphtha lamps, oilcloth and varnish making; the illuminating oils for burning in lamps or stoves; the heavy oils for lubricating and producing paraffin wax, or for gas enrichment, and in Russia to a great extent for fuel; and lastly a residue of coke which is burnt under the still. Nothing is lost, except the unavoidable waste in the process of manufacture. This cannot be said of any other substance in or on the earth. Our metals, for instance, are found in nature as ores, generally oxides, and have to be extracted by some metallurgical process; thus the best iron ores yield only 50 per cent. of metal, and even gold which is found as a metal has to be separated from the sand of the alluvial deposit, or the quartz of the reef in which it is contained.

The loss in the process of distillation is given at 10 per cent. for American and Russian oil, whereas in the distillation of shale oil as much as 30 per cent. is recorded.

In the early days of the petroleum industry the most valuable product was the illuminating oil, and the attention of the manufacturer was directed to the extraction of the largest possible proportion of this product. With a view to the attainment of this object the so-called "cracking" process has been largely adopted. This consists in arranging the dome of the still in such a manner that the vapour of heavier oils rising from the heated liquid condenses and falls back into the oil in the retort. Here it meets with a higher temperature than necessary for volatilization, and is decomposed, giving a larger yield of illuminating oil, and a deposit of carbon. This process, which has given such good results, is said to have been discovered by mere accident. A still-man at a refinery at Newark, New Jersey, left his still at a time when the distillate indicated 43° gravity, with a tendency to increase, intending to return in half-an-hour to cut off the remaining portion of the outflow into the heavy oil-tank, but was detained by sudden illness for four hours. When he returned he found a small stream of light-coloured oil passing over, with a gravity of 48°. This unexpected and abnormal occurrence led to experiments being carried out which showed that the upper part of the still had become sufficiently cooled to condense the vapour, and that the oil thus formed became decomposed or "cracked" in contact with the hot fluid in the retort, with the result of an increased production of kerosene, and in consequence stills were constructed in such a way as to carry out this reaction as a special process.

The great heat necessary to volatilize the heavier

hydrocarbons has an injurious effect on the colour and odour of the distillate. With a view to reducing the temperature efforts have been made to distil under reduced pressure, that is, by applying a vacuum pump in a manner similar to that adopted in the manufacture of sugar. This process has not, however, been generally successful. Recently a vacuum still has been patented by Messrs. Wanklyn and Cooper in this country, in which the vacuum is produced not by a pump, but by a vertical pipe 40 feet in length, into which the distillate flows, and which has for effect to enable the distillation to be carried on in approximate vacuum. This still has not yet been used on a large scale. I have given a cursory outline of the general system of separating the various hydrocarbons contained in crude petroleum. A description of the methods adopted to purify and bleach the various distillates would be beyond the scope of this pamphlet.

CHAPTER VI

In past times petroleum was collected at the outcrops, where it flowed to the surface in small quantities, or, as in America, collected by the aborigines by spreading their blankets on the streams which carried small quantities of the oil on the surface of the water. In Hanover pot-holes were dug where the oil collected, and in Galicia shafts were sunk and the oil raised to the surface in buckets by hand. At the present day in some localities, as for instance in Mexico, the same rude process is followed, and pot-holes are dug near the natural outflow of the oil, where it collects and is then recovered by the natives and used ·either for burning in open lamps or for medicinal purposes. The shafts were succeeded by bore-holes, put down by hand to moderate depths, and the oil scooped up by means of long tubes with a valve at one end. By the application of the steam-engine to the boring apparatus great depths were attained, the drilling was performed at a much more rapid rate, and at less cost. The apparatus used is similar in principle, though differing greatly in detail, in different countries. These differences are dictated by the necessities of the existing circumstances.

An apparatus which acts satisfactorily in strata nearly horizontal and not very hard, would not be applicable in a district where the strata is much contorted or difficult to pierce. The main instrument used in all the apparatus used for boring consists of a cutting-tool or chisel, which has to be raised a certain height and is allowed to fall on the bottom of the bore-hole, when by the force of the blow thus occasioned it cuts into the strata. The up-and-down movement is caused by a mechanical arrangement on the surface connected with a small steam-engine. This chisel or cutting-tool is connected with the surface by means of iron rods, or wooden poles, or a rope. In hand-drilling, iron rods were and are to this day invariably used for all kinds of boring. In the United States the iron rods were soon replaced by the rope, and in Canada by the wooden poles. On the continent of Europe the iron rods are still generally used for all kinds of borings, including petroleum, although the Canadian system has been successfully introduced in Hanover and Elsass (Germany), and in Galicia (Austria).

The arrangement of what the driller terms a "set of tools" is somewhat different when iron rods are used, or ropes and poles. In the former case the chisel with its connecting pieces is lifted up by a contrivance called a freefall tool, and allowed to drop a certain height, usually from two to three feet, and the force of the blow is equal to the weight of the tools—about 18 cwt.—multiplied by the distance of the fall. When rope or wooden poles are used, the chisel is attached to a sliding-piece termed "jars" by the drillers, which has the effect of taking off the jar on the apparatus caused by the blow of the tools on the bottom of the bore-hole.

In the United States petroleum-well boring has been brought to great perfection. Several thousand wells are bored every year for oil, and to depths down to 3000 feet, at a comparatively small cost. The outlay for a well 1500 feet deep is usually estimated at about £800, including the engine and boiler and all labour. These wells are bored with great rapidity unless the work is impeded through accidental circumstances, and in the usual course a well is finished within three months. The American system has been introduced in the Baku oil-field, but has not met with unqualified success. Owing to the nature of the strata and the condition of the oil, which is thick and mixed with sand, the oil has to be raised by means of scoops, and in consequence the wells have to be drilled with a diameter of eighteen inches, for which the Fabian freefall system is preferable to the American jars. The lining-pipes in the Russian field, although made of sheet-iron, represent a serious item in the cost, owing to the wide diameter.

The Canadian method of boring is substantially the same as the American, with the difference that wooden poles are used instead of the rope. These poles are joined together by conical screws, which have to be screwed and unscrewed in lowering or raising the tools, which causes great loss of time. Nevertheless, in Canada the drillers are able to complete one hundred feet of boring in a day, which is a very satisfactory result.

Either of these systems is preferable, in regard to time occupied in boring, to the more antiquated method with heavy iron rods, as these cannot be raised or lowered with the rapidity with which a rope or the light Canadian poles can be moved.

By whatever method the well is bored and the oil strata attained, the next operation is to line the well, if necessary. It is always usual to put in a certain length of casing to keep out the surface water, but in many districts, notably in America, it is not necessary to case the entire well. This is a considerable saving in cost. In most petroleum districts the nature of the ground requires the well to be cased from top to bottom. This is generally done with wrought-iron lap-welded tubing, with screw joints. Sometimes, however, the casing is made of sheet-iron, riveted, which is more economical but not so durable.

As soon as the well is completed, a small pump specially constructed for the purpose of raising a liquid containing considerable quantities of gas is put in, unless the oil flows. When the oil-bearing strata is first tapped, it frequently happens that owing to the force of the confined gas a regular outburst takes place, and millions of gallons of oil are thrown up in the shape of a fountain. However, in a short time this effect subsides, and eventually the pump has to be put in. When a well yields large quantities of oil, that is, from fifty to several hundred barrels a day, a separate engine is applied, but when, as in most instances, only a few barrels are to be raised, a central engine is erected, from which the wells are pumped or "rocked," in the language of the Canadian driller. The oil from the different wells is then concentrated by means of connecting pipes with a central tank or tanks, from which it is conveyed to the refinery.

CHAPTER VII

STORAGE AND TRANSPORT

THE rapid development of the means for storage and transport of oil necessary to meet the large quantities raised and bring it to market at a reasonable cost, is one of the most interesting features connected with this remarkable industry. At first the crude oil was put into barrels and carted away from the mine to the nearest railway-station, and this is still done at the present time in some districts. Then the tank-car was introduced, by which oil in bulk could be transported, each car holding 60 to 100 barrels. But at present, in all the great producing districts the oil is forced for miles through pipelines, and in the United States there are over 15,000 miles of pipe-line laid down, connected with storage-tanks holding some 40,000,000 barrels. The oil raised in Pennsylvania is collected at central tank-stations, and then forced through six-inch pipes up to New York, where it is refined. The pipe-line from Oban to New York is 312 miles in length, with twelve pumping-stations, giving an average of 26 miles to each engine. In the United States, the tanks in the producing districts are of wrought-iron, circular, and hold up to 10,000 barrels of oil. These tanks are placed on brick supports about two feet from the ground, which enables them to be easily examined with a view to detecting leakage. The tanks in the petroleum districts of Pennsylvania are usually placed in sets of four to ten in fields as remote as possible from habitations or other buildings, and they present a somewhat dismal and forbidding aspect. Each tank is provided with a suitable gauge, and the quantity it contains is accurately measured every day. Very few accidents have occurred, owing to the great precautions which are observed. The writer was informed that in case a tank became ignited through some mischance, the fire was extinguished by firing blank cartridges out of a cannon at the flame, and this appears quite natural, as we know that the vibration caused by snapping a cap on a gun is sufficient to extinguish a lighted candle at a distance of several feet. Petroleum reservoirs are frequently placed underground, and sometimes constructed of brick or timber, lined with clay. But experience gives the preference to the wrought-iron tank for the storage of large quantities. Small reservoirs holding 500 to 1000 barrels may be made of timber in shape something like large barrels, well caulked and pitched inside. Some of the iron storage-tanks erected for storing oil on the wharves on the Thames hold nearly 1,000,000 gallons. I am indebted to Mr. A. G. Tait, the Westminster representative of the Pearson and Knowles Coal and Iron Co., Limited, for details of three petroleum storage-tanks erected for the Tank Storage and Carriage Company at Purfleet. These are 89 ft. 3 in. in diameter, by 25 ft.

6 in. in height, and have a capacity of 997,000 gallons, and are, I believe, the largest constructed in this country. The oil is pumped out of the ship into the tanks at the rate of 1000 barrels per hour. From the tanks it is transferred to barrels or tank-carts for distribution. The latter were introduced in 1889.

The transport by sea has of late years undergone a great change. Previous to 1878 the American petroleum was carried in barrels, but in that year the transport in bulk was tried on the Atlantic in sailing-ships. Since then the tank-steamers have been introduced, and in 1886 the first was constructed on the Tyne, carrying 3000 tons of liquid cargo. These ships contain seven to nine compartments or tanks, each holding about 4000 barrels, and are separated from the engines and boilers by a safety-well or empty space, sometimes filled with water, and the total number of barrels thus carried varies from 28,000 to 36,000, representing a weight of about 4000 to 5000 tons. Every precaution is taken to render the transport safe in the way of expansion trunks, ventilating-pipes, etc. These steamers are capable of attaining a speed of eleven knots per hour, and, strange to say, as a rule burn coal as fuel. There are at present a great number of these steamers engaged in the trade of transporting petroleum, and it is remarkable that so few accidents have occurred in the service. The accidents which have been recorded are minutely described by Mr. Boverton Redwood, in his paper on "The Transport of Petroleum in Bulk" read before the Institution of Civil Engineers, and these have nearly all taken place in harbour. The explosions and fires on board tank-steamers have been clearly ascertained in nine cases out of ten to have been caused by carelessness or ignorance. It must, however, be stated that the steamship *Lux* was lost in the Doro Channel, Grecian Archipelago, through fire during stormy weather, and Mr. Redwood attributes this accident to " the escape of oil from the expansion trunk of the cargo-tanks into the port-side bunker, and the overflow of such escaping oil through the bunker into the stokehole where, or in the bilges, it became ignited." The steamship *Lux* carried a cargo of Russian refined petroleum; but most of the accidents which have occurred to steamers carrying petroleum in bulk have been when the cargo has consisted of crude oil. This is easily explained by the presence of the light hydrocarbons and gas in the crude which are eliminated from the refined oil by the process of distillation. We have seen that the quantity of petroleum of various qualities imported into this country in the year 1893 was over 155,000,000 gallons, nearly all of which would be carried by tank-steamers representing a freight capacity of about 550,000 tons.

This large quantity of petroleum is distributed in this country mostly in tank-cars to the larger towns, and retailed in tank-carts. The obsolete barrel, however, is still to be found in small towns and villages, and on the hawkers' carts in the metropolis.

CHAPTER VIII

LIQUID FUEL

FROM the preceding cursory glance at the known oil-fields of the world, it is evident that the quantity of petroleum in different parts of the earth must be immense, and if entirely converted into kerosene there would be enough to light up the globe for centuries to come. But mineral oil is destined to play another important part in the economy of the world, in becoming the fuel of the future. It has been quite sufficiently experimented with to demonstrate that it is practically perfectly applicable and safe for all heating purposes. At present the production is not sufficient to enable it to come into competition with coal, but when we remember the immense reserves known to exist, the time must come when the further development of these important resources will place an enormous quantity of liquid fuel on the markets of the world. At present the total production is difficult to estimate, owing to want of authentic records from many countries; but it may be approximately taken at about 100,000,000 barrels of crude oil. This produce is at present refined, and it may be safely assumed that the total production of kerosene is about 40,000,000 barrels. The other products consist of light oils, lubricating oils, and residue; the latter constitutes the liquid fuel. It is, however, almost exclusively produced in Russia, and amounts to over 3,000,000 tons, and assuming a ton of residue to equal in calorific effect two tons of coal, we have at present a production of liquid fuel equal to 6,000,000 or 7,000,000 tons of coal—a very insignificant quantity as compared with the consumption of coal in the world. In order to compete as a fuel, the production of petroleum will have to be greatly increased, and, as far as this country is concerned, this increased production will have to come from fields lying on the sea-coast, where it can be shipped in tank-steamers and brought to the consumer at a reasonable cost.

The idea of applying liquid fuel in the place of coal is by no means a recent one. Many years ago it was proposed to use it in the Royal Navy, and Admiral Selwyn made elaborate experiments, and strongly advocated its advantages for ships of war. It may, however, be said to have been practically applied first by Mr. Urquhart on the locomotives in Southern Russia, and about the same time on the steamers employed in the Caspian Sea for the transport of petroleum from Baku to the Volga. The principle on which the liquid fuel is burnt in locomotives or steamships consists in breaking or pulverizing the liquid fuel by means of a jet of steam, and all the different inventions for the use of liquid fuel may be described as modifications of this idea.

In a paper read by Mr. G. Stockfleth, at the Society of Arts, on May 20, 1894, he thus describes the process as adopted in Russia.

" Many injectors or pulverizators in Russia, called
fasunkas, have been constructed and patented, but it has
been found that the most primitively constructed pulverizators answer as well as the more complicated kinds.
The apparatus used under the stills consists simply of two
half-inch pipes, one leading the oil from a tank, the other
steam from a boiler. The ends of the pipes are flattened
by a blow of a hammer, and then tied together with a
piece of wire; the steam-jet catches the outflowing oil
and forms the spray. It is well to keep the oil a little
warm to facilitate its passage in the pipes through which
it descends by gravitation. This pulverizator gives entire
satisfaction; the flame is powerful and bright, and not a
drop of oil is wasted when once the flow has been regulated. No smoke or flame ascends the chimney—which,
by the way, can be very short—as the steam-jet itself
creates sufficient draught. A somewhat neater appearance
can be given to the injector when the oil-pipe is arranged
inside the steam-pipe, and provided with a cast-iron or
brass nozzle which can be shaped to give the flame any
desired form. As far back as 1880 I had occasion to make,
on behalf of Messrs. Nobel Brothers, in St. Petersburg,
some experiments with oil firing before a committee of the
Russian Admiralty. At that time astatki firing was a
novelty. The object was to demonstrate its practicability
for firing marine boilers. The pulverizator was of a somewhat complicated construction. The results were, however, satisfactory; the boiler used belonged to a steam
launch.

" Experiments have been made with compressed air

for spraying the oil, but the results have not materially differed from those obtained with steam. Air must, of course, in any case, have access to the flame, and openings on the front of the flue must be provided for its admittance. In most cases the hole in the furnace door through which the nozzle of the pulverizator is introduced, is sufficient for letting in the quantity necessary for the combustion. The action of the steam is therefore solely mechanical, and serves only for cutting up the oil into small particles, which being surrounded by the necessary air for their combustion, catch fire before they reach the bottom of the flue. By using steam for spraying, no oil accumulates in the flue when the flow is regulated, consequently a complete combustion of the oil takes place. If better results should be obtainable by using compressed air for spraying, the reason would have to be looked for in some chemical effect of the steam upon the oil which, to some extent, could deprive the latter of its heat-creating properties. There is, however, no probability for this anticipation; if the steam had this effect, it would already have done its work in the still, where superheated steam is admitted into the crude oil to facilitate the distillation of the different crude oil products. Looking at the question from the point of cost, it is not probable that the compressed air can be produced cheaper than the necessary quantity of steam taken direct from the boiler. It is, in fact, but a very small quantity which is necessary for doing this work, when the pulverizator is properly constructed; and no case has come to my knowledge in Russia where the adoption of liquid fuel has augmented the quantities of feed-water used in a perceptible degree. The chief point in the construction of the pulverizátor is to avoid waste of steam, that is to say, to construct the nozzle in such manner that every particle of steam takes care of a corresponding particle of oil. This object will best be secured when the openings for the steam, as well as for the oil, are made long and narrow, and are placed as close to one another as possible. All the different Russian constructions are made in this way. The openings are about $1\frac{1}{4}$ inches long, and $\frac{1}{8}$ inch to $\frac{1}{8}$ inch wide. As the oil sometimes contains paraffin, which is likely to choke this narrow opening, it is essential to have an arrangement by which steam can be led through the oil-passage to clean it out. The rest of the construction may be varied to suit particular cases, and with a view to facilitate and cheapen the manufacture.

"At the present time a great many ships on the Black Sea, and all steamers on the Caspian Sea, as well as all locomotives in Southern Russia, burn astatki. The general advantages obtained by using liquid fuel in any boiler, whether stationary, locomotive, or marine, are the following. It can be adapted to any construction of boiler without material change in the existing arrangement for firing with coal, in fact coal and oil can be used alternatively if so desired. The fire-bars have simply to be taken out or covered with thin slabs and cinders, the furnace door has to be provided with a hole for introducing the nozzle of the pulverizator, and the steam-pipe and oil-pipe have to be connected respectively with the boiler and the oil-tank. The steam-generating power of astatki is considerable; one ton of oil is, in this respect, equal to more than two tons of best steam coal, and is often claimed to be equal even to three tons of coal; it depends, of course, upon the quality of oil and coal used for the comparison. The fire can be extinguished instantaneously, and is absolutely free from smoke or ashes. The frequent opening of the furnace doors can be avoided, thus saving heat and preventing leakage of tubes, due to currents of cold air. Rapidity in raising steam, and complete control over the fire, are secured, thus avoiding waste of steam by the safety-valves, and the boiler pressure can be regulated better than in the case of coal-firing. After mentioning these general advantages a few words may be added about the special advantages accruing to railways and steamships. The valuable spaces at railway-stations, which have now to be sacrificed for accommodating coal supply, could be reduced by about two-thirds, as only half the tonnage would have to be kept in stock, and this quantity can be stored more economically in point of space than the same quantity of coal. A considerable amount of labour employed in storing coal and loading tenders can be saved, and the oil can be taken in simultaneously with the water supply, as quickly and in a like manner. The avoidance of smoke and blowing safety-valves will greatly add to the comfort of the passengers, a point for which the railway companies are usually prepared to make considerable sacrifices.

" The hard work of the stoker on an express train is reduced, as far as firing goes, to simply giving the regulating valve of the injector a turn from time to time, and the absence of dirt and smoke makes the service less disagreeable than with coal-firing.

"For steamships, the advantages of using liquid fuel are of still greater importance. Much valuable space which has now to be sacrificed for the coal-bunkers can be saved; the oil can be kept in ballast-tanks at the bottom of the ship, an arrangement which greatly augments the stability of the vessel, and the oil can gradually, as it is consumed, be replaced by water. The size of the stoke-hole can be reduced considerably, and the number of stokers diminished in the proportion of one to four. In stormy weather, and in case water should gain access to the stokehole and put the fire out, it is considerably more troublesome and takes more time to re-light a coal fire than to re-start the oil fire, and the risk of accidents by scalding is diminished. The danger of fire in the coal-bunkers will not be replaced by any similar risk connected with the use of oil."

With reference to the use of liquid fuel on locomotives, it is interesting to refer to the results obtained by Mr. James Holden, locomotive superintendent of the Great Eastern Railway, by the process invented and adopted by him. On the locomotives using liquid fuel there is an absence of constant and laborious firing; the requisite pressure of steam is easily obtained by an almost imperceptible movement of the injector valve, there is an absence of smoke, and a great uniformity of pressure. Mr. Goodwin, in his inaugural address as President of the Society of Engineers in February 1894, gave a description of these locomotives, and their working cost, and stated that an express engine using 35·4 lbs. of coal per mile, consumed under similar circumstances 11·8 lbs. of coal and 10·5 lbs. of liquid fuel, or a total of 22·3 lbs. of fuel; and assuming the liquid fuel to be equal in calorific effect to double its weight of coal, that is, $10·5 \times 2 = 21$ lbs. of coal, the total consumption, namely, 32·8 lbs., would be less than the ordinary consumption of coal. The advantages of this system are summed up as follows. First, with an ordinary grate steam can be easily raised without working the injector; secondly, fuel can be interchanged according to the state of the market; thirdly, with a thin coal fire oil can be shut off at will without running the risk of chilling the fire-box; fourthly, when standing the coal fire will maintain steam. For several years a number of locomotive engines on the Great Eastern Railway have used liquid fuel, and one of these engines is recorded to have travelled 47,000 miles without a single failure or accident. The great difficulty in extending the use of liquid fuel in England is the impossibility of obtaining a sufficient supply at a low cost, otherwise it would be very generally used, considering the great calorific effect and the practical advantages of its application. The primary advantage in using liquid fuel lies in its great calorific value, which is due to its composition, namely, a mixture of hydrocarbons of various densities.

In the United States the average composition of crude oil is taken at 86 per cent. of carbon and 14 per cent. of hydrogen, and the calorific value at 21,192 British heat-units as compared with coal yielding 14,500 heat-units. In practice it is found that petroleum refuse gives a comparatively better result than its theoretical value. This has been sometimes erroneously attributed to the action of decomposing steam supplied by the jet to spray the oil. But any effect of this kind is an impossibility, because if the steam were decomposed into its constituent elements an absorption of heat would take place, in order to liberate the hydrogen equal to that produced by the re-combination with oxygen, and no effective result, as far as a development of heat, would be obtained. The great calorific effect of liquid hydrocarbons must be attributed to other causes. Experiments upon the calorific value of coal show that the heating power of coal is greater than the theoretical value of the constituent elements, and this must also be so in the case of hydrocarbons.

Be this as it may, the results obtained in practice show that in round figures one ton of liquid fuel properly burnt for heating purposes will be equal to two tons of ordinary coal. The experience gained up to the present time in the use of liquid fuel establishes the following facts—

1. That it is a safe and economically manipulated substance.

2. That its calorific value is much greater than coal, and consequently it offers advantages of requiring less room for storage.

3. That its cost at present delivered in England is forty shillings per ton, equal to two tons of coal in practical effect.

4. That the supply has to be obtained from foreign countries, and that the price is unstable.

There is one great advantage in the use of liquid fuel in

locomotives which has not been sufficiently brought forward, and that is the diminished weight to be carried, which would enable the locomotive to travel many more miles without stopping for a fresh supply of fuel. The introduction of the water-troughs by Mr. Ramsbottom on the London and North-Western Railway was attended with most beneficial results, by enabling trains to run for long distances without stopping to take in water, and a similar advantage would follow the adoption of liquid fuel on railways.

Considering that liquid fuel if properly consumed in a locomotive does not emit either smoke or noxious vapours, it seems surprising that it has not been adopted on our underground railways. There must be some reason for this; perhaps the frequent stoppages may be supposed to interfere with the combustion, and yet one would think that any mechanical difficulties could be overcome. It is certain that if a smokeless fuel could be adopted in the tunnels of the underground railways instead of the sulphurous coke at present used, it would be a great comfort to the millions of passengers who travel by these lines.

The heavier grades of petroleum distillates have recently been applied to the enrichment of gas in this country. The idea of using petroleum for the production or enrichment of gas is not new. Attempts to enrich water-gas date as far back as 1824, and a process for the manufacture of high standard gas direct from petroleum was introduced in this country in 1846. There are several systems by which petroleum is retorted, so that the oil is

subjected to a heat of about 1600° Fahr., and thus trans-
formed into gas, leaving liquid and solid residuals, one of
the best known being that of Pintsch, but this process is
generally applied to the preparation of gas for compression.
The process of manufacturing what is termed carburetted
water-gas, which has been in use in the United States
for some time, was introduced into this country only three
years ago, but since then has been rapidly developed.
The primary reason for the use of petroleum in the manufacture of gas lies in the high price of cannel coal, which is
generally used in order to bring the gas up to the legal
illuminating standard. The process of manufacturing carburetted water-gas consists in decomposing steam by
passing it through incandescent coke, thus producing
hydrogen and carbonic oxide, and forming what is denom-
inated "water-gas," which in burning produces great heat
but gives very little light. In order to bring it up to the
necessary illuminating power it is charged with a certain
quantity of carburetted hydrogen, in the shape of petroleum
which is gasified and rendered permanent in suitable
apparatus. The process adopted in this country is the
Howe process, by which less than four gallons of oil is
required per 1000 cubic feet of gas to bring it up to an
illuminating power equal to 20 candles. The kind of oil
generally used is that which is known as Russian solar
distillate, being a product passing out of the still after the
kerosene or illuminating oil has been extracted, and before
the lubricating oil is distilled over. But other grades of
oil from America and Scotland have also been successfully
applied. The total quantity of oil of different kinds at

present consumed in this country in the manufacture of gas may be estimated at from 15 to 20 millions of gallons a year.

It has been stated that the Fire Brigade Committee of the London County Council propose to try the experimental use of oil fuel in one of the fire-engines. The idea seems to be that the use of liquid fuel would be convenient more especially on the river fire appliances.

CHAPTER IX

THE FLASHING POINT AND LAMP ACCIDENTS

THE temperature at which petroleum oil for ordinary use ought not to give off inflammable vapour is termed the safe flashing point, and this degree of heat has been for some years a matter of discussion, not to say contention. Originally the limit of safety was fixed at 100° Fahr. open test, that is to say, that any oil which heated up to that temperature gave off inflammable vapour in the open air was considered unsafe, the reason for this limit being that very rarely in this climate the temperature of the atmosphere in the shade reaches that degree, and this test was fixed by the legislature.

The first Act of Parliament referring to petroleum was passed in 1862, soon after the introduction of illuminating oil from the United States. In this Act petroleum was defined to include any product thereof which "gives off an inflammable vapour at a temperature of less than 100° Fahr." But no special method of testing was prescribed by which the degree of inflammability was to be determined. The next Act, passed in 1868, contained a detailed system of testing by which the degree of inflammability was to be determined, and it was enacted to

include certain other specified oils and products which
gave off an inflammable vapour under 100° Fahr. The
apparatus adopted for testing was as follows:—A few
ounces of the liquid to be tested were put in a small
metal cup, provided with a flat rim and raised edges a
quarter of an inch high, which was placed in a larger
vessel containing water, under which was a spirit-lamp.
A thermometer was placed in the oil, which became
gradually heated by the water-bath. A fine wire was
fixed to or resting on the edge, which was thus a quarter
of an inch above the rim, and a very small flame was then
passed along this wire, and the temperature carefully
noted at which an explosion of the vapours took place.
The apparatus was surrounded by a screen to prevent
currents of air interfering with the results. This apparatus was not satisfactory, and so many discrepancies
occurred between tests made by different operators that it
was felt by the trade that some other method of testing
ought to be adopted. This led to the invention of the
close-test apparatus by Sir Frederick Abel, which was
introduced into the Petroleum Act of 1879. The flashing
point of 100° Fahr. with the old open test was taken as
the basis, but replaced by its equivalent, 73° Fahr., by
the new Abel close test. Previous to this Act, another
one, namely, in 1871, had been passed, and when introduced as a bill contained a form of close test, but with a
flashing point of 85° Fahr. The petroleum trade desired
to have the flashing point fixed as low as possible, whereas
the paraffin trade and the Metropolitan Board of Works
were anxious to see it higher than the existing regulation.

The opposition to the 85° Fahr. flashing point was so great that the clause was left out of the Act. Although several attempts were made to rectify this omission by inserting a test of 82 degrees, these were not successful, and at present the test remains at 73° Fahr. In a proposed Bill in 1888 this test was not changed. The object of all these Acts is to regulate the storing and conveyance of inflammable liquids in order to insure public safety, and stringent regulations have to be observed in the handling of such liquids having what is considered a dangerous flashing point—that is to say, giving off inflammable vapour at a temperature which may be realized under ordinary circumstances in this climate. Therefore the petroleum or other inflammable liquids which come under the Act are such as have a flashing point under 73° Fahr., which is considered the safe limit, and no regulation whatever is provided under the present Act for what is called high-test petroleum—namely, that which does not flash at 73° in Abel's close test. In a bill which was mooted and discussed in 1888, it was proposed to compel the so-called "safe oil," namely that having a high flashing point, to be stored on registered premises, except as to retail traders, who were, however, limited to sixty gallons of safe oil, three gallons of petroleum spirit, and ten gallons of petroleum and spirit combined. This Bill was founded on extended inquiries and conferences with the trade, which had been suggested by the Select Committee of 1883, and it was introduced and read a first time in the House of Commons on February 9, 1891, but never got any further. The effect of the Bill was not, however, to alter the flashing point, but to introduce some regulations for the storage of the safe oils in large quantities.

That some excuse for legislation in this direction exists must be admitted when we consider that the present storage of safe petroleum at the wharfs must be about 600,000 barrels, equal to 20,000,000 gallons. The petroleum trade is opposed to legislation in this direction, except as far as safety, as involving possibly a further outlay on the present costly installations for the storage of petroleum at the wharves. Any alteration of the flashing point as at present fixed would not generally be acceptable, nor is any alteration necessary, for the accidents caused by safe illuminating oil, other than those attributable to negligence, are few among the list of such occurrences.

Nevertheless, the subject of the safe storage and transport of an inflammable liquid like petroleum oil is one which demands the attention of the legislature. Last year a Select Committee of the House of Commons was appointed to inquire into the matter, and held a few sittings. The evidence which has been given so far tends to show that the danger in burning mineral oil as an illuminant lies more in the use of defective lamps than in the flashing point of the oil. In 1893 there were 456 fires recorded in London as having occurred through lamp accidents, and the great majority of these were caused by the chance upsetting of the lamps; and in 1894 out of seventy-three fires attended with loss of life, twenty-seven were caused by mineral oil lamp accidents, involving the loss of thirty-two lives. The faulty construction of the lamps was pointed out by Mr. Spencer in his evidence, and certainly the cheap foreign lamp as sold in this country is constructed in a way almost to court misfortune. Generally these cheap lamps are furnished with a glass or porcelain reservoir, which breaks when upset, and then the petroleum oil spreads and ignites at the burning wick. Therefore it is suggested that the use of fragile reservoirs ought to be disallowed. Again, in the common lamps, as at present in use, the flame of the wick is not in any way protected from the petroleum vapour which may be in the reservoir above the level of the oil. This case is almost similar to an open light in a fiery coal-mine. In order to obviate the danger, safety lamps have been invented to protect the open flame from the vapour, not by a wire gauze, but by enclosing the wick in a metal tube descending to the bottom of the reservoir through the oil, thus shutting off communication between the vapour and the flame of the wick. With such improvements in the construction of lamps it is anticipated that accidents caused by petroleum oil will be seldom recorded. The subject of petroleum lamps was fully considered by Mr. Boverton Redwood in his admirable Cantor lectures some years ago, and there is not much to add to what he then said.

The last development in lamps is perhaps the burning of petroleum vapour instead of the oil itself. A lamp has been recently introduced in Germany, in which the oil is allowed to drop from a small reservoir in the upper part of the lamp into a vapourizing chamber heated by the

flame of the burning oil vapour. The initial heat to light
the lamp is produced by introducing at first a small
quantity of spirit. The light is very powerful, and it is
proposed to adopt these lamps for use in large structures,
such as railway-stations, and also for street lighting.

It must be pointed out that accidents caused by petroleum lamps are frequently erroneously attributed to
explosions of vapour in the reservoirs. Such explosions
do sometimes take place, although Professor Lambert
doubts their occurrence altogether. The following case of
a lamp explosion came within the writer's knowledge.
On a winter's evening three persons were sitting round a
table on which stood a common petroleum lamp, which
had been burning for about five hours, when it suddenly
exploded without being moved or touched. The frag-
ments of glass were blown in every direction, and the
burning wick dropped on the table, where it was promptly
extinguished. No oil appeared to have been spilt, and
the reservoir must have been empty, and under the circumstances would become filled with a mixture of air and
vapour sufficient to cause an explosion. It is needless
to point out that the lamp had been unintentionally placed
in a dangerous condition. Such explosions are, however,
rare. In general, lamp disasters are the result of accidental upsetting of the lamp, and in such cases the
flashing point is not an important factor. That is to say,
a petroleum oil of high flashing point under such circumstances will ignite at the burning wick. The analysis of
the usual run of lamp accidents tends to show that the
most important requirements to prevent such occurrences

are, first, a lamp made of metal which will not easily
be broken, and secondly, some safety contrivance to prevent contact of the vapour in the reservoir with the flame
of the wick.

This is clearly pointed out in the circular of the London
County Council on petroleum lamps, containing suggestions "partly founded on recommendations made by
Sir Frederick Abel, C.B., D.C.L., F.R.S., and Mr. Boverton
Redwood, F.I.C., F.C.S., after investigating the causes of
lamp accidents." The circular states that the wick should
be enclosed in a thin sheet of metal tube open at the
bottom, which should reach almost to the bottom of the
reservoir. That the oil reservoirs should be made of
metal without any opening other than that into which the
upper part of the lamp is screwed, and that every lamp
should have a proper extinguishing apparatus. If these
suggestions were universally carried out lamp accidents
would be of rare occurrence. But, as Mr. Alfred Spencer
pointed out in his evidence before the Committee of the
House of Commons, the London County Council may
make suggestions, but has no power to enforce them.

It must be added that a great number of the accidents
attributed to petroleum are caused by misuse and carelessness. Among the former is the very reprehensible practice
of pouring petroleum oil on the coals in a grate when
lighting a fire, in order to make it burn up quicker. The
following is one out of numerous cases recorded in the
daily press—

"A girl, while kindling a fire at an early hour yesterday
morning, poured some paraffin oil on the fuel to make it

burn. The flames shot out and caught her clothes, setting them on fire. She ran screaming into the passage, and her cries attracted her employer and some passers-by. Before medical aid could arrive she died in great agony from the effects of the burns."

Another frequent cause of accident arises from the use of the small penny lamps. Not long ago a child three years old was burnt to death through playing with one of these lamps which had carelessly been left within its reach.

It would be difficult to prevent such want of prudence by Act of Parliament, and all that can be done is to warn people of the danger they run in misusing petroleum in this manner. Fatal accidents from these causes have been so frequent that it cannot be out of place here to revert pointedly to the danger of using petroleum oil in a way and for purposes for which it is not applicable.

CHAPTER X

PETROLEUM ENGINES

[*Contributed by* MR. ARTHUR ROWAN, A.M.I.C.E.]

THESE engines are the latest adaptation of means to extract from petroleum the energy which lies latent in it. As compared with gas-engines and steam-engines they are still in process of development, but should the future bear out their present promise of freedom from danger and simplicity of action, it is not too much to expect that they will be one of the most important, if not *the* most important factor in the demand for petroleum, just as the steam-engine is now the most important factor in the demand for coal.

The gas-engine in its limited field has shown what a demand for handy small-power engines exists; and the annual consumption of coal-gas has been increased by many thousands of millions of cubic feet owing to their invention.

But the field for the petroleum engine is unlimited. It is an easy calculation that 100,000 engines of only 5 horse-power each would require an annual supply of 200,000,000 gallons of refined oil to keep them at full work. When it is considered that it is quite possible that before twenty years have passed two or three hundred thousand petroleum engines may be at work in Europe, the power-user may well begin to inquire where is the oil coming from. Mr. Boyd has already given the answer, to which the reader can refer.

Before going further it will be necessary for the sake of brevity and clearness to define in some way the name " petroleum engine."

The word petroleum is used in England in the loosest manner. The residues of petroleum refineries are constantly referred to as crude petroleum, whereas crude petroleum is really an almost unknown product in this country. A good deal of confusion has also been caused in the minds of many commercial power-users by constant references in journals and books to petroleum as fuel. The progress of petroleum by distillation from its raw or crude state to the well-known commercial products which are in daily use is roughly as follows—

1. *Crude:* Inflammable at very low temperatures; may not be shipped or stored without special precautions; is not at present available for use in petroleum engines. 2. *Volatile oils:* Often sold as petroleum spirit or petroleum essence; are dangerously inflammable; much used to carburet air for "so-called" petroleum engines. 3. *Oils for domestic use:* Are known by different names, such as kerosene, tea-rose, russolene, daylight, etc., etc.; being distilled and refined can be burnt inside the cylinders of internal combustion engines without clogging. 4. *Heavy viscid oils:* Require a high temperature to gasify; are very little used as yet for petroleum engines. 5. *Residues.*

Petroleum (4 and 5 in above classification) can be and is used in favourable localities as a fuel to heat furnaces and boilers, and to produce steam.

The use of petroleum in petroleum engines is an entirely different proceeding, requiring another class of oil, and is conducted on totally different principles.

In the following pages the words "petroleum engine" will mean an engine driven by the *explosion* of refined mineral oil, such as may be legally used in England for domestic consumption in lamps, stoves, etc., that is to say, with a flashing point of 73° Fahr. (close test), and of a specific gravity between ·80 and ·85.

Other engines which use the lighter volatile products of petroleum refineries (Class 2 above), such as benzine, naphtha, and gasoline, I shall refer to as "so-called" oil-engines.

This is a very important distinction to power-users, because the technical conditions and performances of these "so-called" oil-engines are often held up for comparison with the petroleum engine. They were the forerunners of the present commercial petroleum engine. They are often good and economical engines, and very useful in their proper place, but their field must always be a very limited one, because in every civilized country severe legal restrictions are in force concerning the storage and sale of the fuel which they use. With the improvement of the petroleum engine their use may be expected to die out, except in certain countries where oil-refining is carried out on a large scale, and the minor products must be utilized in some form.

These volatile oils are so well adapted for the manufacture of carburetted air, that, if the price of the oils is sufficiently low, there will always be found power-users to take the risk of their use. About 16 per cent. of American crude mineral oil consists of these volatile oils, which must be run off before the lamp oil is obtained, so that a largely increased demand for lamp oil entails a largely increased supply of the volatile oils.

It is quite outside the scope of this pamphlet to explain the chemical and dynamical actions of the forces utilized in the petroleum engine. Suffice it to say here that it is an "internal explosion" engine. To explain this term I may perhaps be permitted to take a cannon as a crude analogy universally known. The cartridge chamber represents the engine cylinder, the cannon ball represents the piston in the cylinder, while the explosive powder in the cannon is represented by a mixture of oil and air in the engine. A small quantity of oil, intimately mixed with a certain quantity of air, forms an explosive, more or less powerful according to the nature of the mixture, and this explosive has great practical advantages over gunpowder and other explosives, because both the constituents can be handled or transported, or stored, without the smallest risk, while one (air) costs nothing, and the other (oil) costs very little. Also the power and rate of burning can be accurately graduated by mixing the two substances in due proportions. For example, one part of oil and four of air would give a quick, powerful explosion, while one part of oil to forty of air would be feeble and slow.

Although in petroleum engines every maker uses an explosive charge of oil and air in the cylinder as the motive force, yet the explosion is obtained by methods varying widely not only in detail but also in principle. Two great divisions in principle may be emphasized without going into technicalities: (1) Where the oil is mechanically divided and intimately mixed with air before explosion; (2) where the oil constituents are chemically dissociated, and are converted wholly or partly into true gases before mixture with air and explosion.

But it is not sufficient merely to obtain an explosion as in a cannon. In a petroleum engine explosions must follow each other rapidly and regularly, while their force and rapidity must be either automatically controlled, or capable of mechanical adjustment according to the power which the engine is called upon to exert at a given moment.

Further, the power derived from the motion of the piston in the cylinder has to be divided, the minor part doing the interior work required by the engine itself, such as compressing air, pumping oil, imparting heat where required, overcoming friction of moving parts, etc.; while the major part is transmitted to the exterior useful work, of whatever kind required.

This being the case, it is evident that the more the interior work is diminished the greater is the amount of force available for useful work. Therefore it is the aim of every manufacturer and designer (1) to get the maximum energy possible on the piston, consistent with the economy of fuel and material; (2) to govern the force produced; (3) to reduce the interior work of the engine. To effect these objects great variety of design is employed by different makers.

The great majority of engines hitherto made have only one cylinder, and work on the so-called "Otto" cycle, which gives one explosion and impulse at every second revolution of the crank. A good many are, however, working with twin cylinders. These obtain an impulse every revolution, while a few large marine engines between 75 and 105 horse-power are double-acting, that is to say, they obtain two impulses to every revolution of the crank.

In some engines the necessary quantities of air and oil are injected or sucked into the cylinder together, then compressed and fired. In some the air only is compressed, and the oil charge in its chemically or mechanically sub-divided state is injected just before ignition. Some makers heat the air before admission to the cylinder, some warm it, some admit it cold.

In some engines the oil is forced into the cylinders by pressure varying in different engines from 8 lbs. to 75 lbs. to the square inch; in others it is merely sucked in by the motion of the piston in the cylinder. Ignition of the charge at the right moment is effected by widely varying means. In some by an electric spark, in some by a red-hot tube, in some by a naked flame, and in some by the heat of the preceding explosion.

The reader who wishes to study the subject, and appreciate the infinite ingenuity and care bestowed on these details, will find various elaborate treatises published on the subject within the last three years, and many special articles on the same subject in the technical journals.   So far as the general public and the petroleum industry are concerned, it is sufficient to know that several of these designs have passed out of the experimental stage into the commercial, and have worked smoothly and successfully for years.

The mechanical difficulties being conquered, rapid development both in size and efficiency must follow. Each type of engine will find its most fitting market. In out-of-the-way spots, economy of fuel will be sacrificed to simplicity of construction ; where artisans and workshops are plentiful, simplicity may well be sacrificed to economy of fuel.

The prime cost is at present a stumbling-block in the way of many small power-users, but with an increased demand and more numerous orders, prices will fall.

It is a curious fact that the price of these engines remains relatively high, although the supply apparently far exceeds the demand.   Over thirty large engineering shops in Europe are engaged in the manufacture, while the patents applied for in 1894, for "Improvements in Oil-engines," may be numbered by hundreds.

This relation between supply and demand might be explained in various ways.   I shall content myself with pointing out the causes which are actually creating or may be expected to create a rapid increase in the demand.

A glance at the catalogues of well-known manufacturers will show at once many causes " claimed."

No boiler.

No external-fire.

No sparks or lights of any kind.

No coal or coke required.

Absolutely free from danger.

No driver required.

Started in five minutes.

No water consumed.

Self-contained.

More efficient than any other engine.

More economical than any other engine.

All these claims and others may be grouped under the three heads of *relative safety*, *relative convenience*, and *relative economy*, as in comparison with gas- and steam-engines; and it will be of interest to follow out as briefly as possible some of the reasons and facts on which these claims are based. If they are well founded, then the demand is insured, and with the demand will follow the fall in price which the petroleum industry desires.

Relative safety.—There is no doubt that the petroleum engine has advantages. A carefully-driven and well-maintained steam-engine is safe, but the safety depends on the driver. His absence or negligence may lead to disastrous explosions.

This is a truism, but an extract from a very recent case, recording the opinion of H.M. Inspector of Factories, shows that it cannot be repeated too often.

"MAJOR VAUGHAN: Unfortunately, this employment "of boys to look after engines is very common at these "small factories. The Home Office is not able to interfere.

F

"Judge French: Is no certificate of competence "required of an engineer in charge of an engine? With "an incompetent man or ignorant boy, the lives of all the "workmen on the premises are endangered.

"Major Vaughan: No, not under the Factory Act. "I often call the attention of the employers to the fact that "boys are engaged in such work.

"Judge French: What is the use of appealing to "such employers? You should impress the danger of the "system on the Home Office. I hope you will report this "to your Department. Under the Mines Act, a certificate "of competency is required of engineers; the Home Office "might be induced to extend the system to Factories."

With coal-gas engines supplied from a main, when the ignition is by naked flame, a certain amount of risk, though it be small, must always be connected; but a well-designed petroleum engine has all the elements of safety. If the attendant is negligent or absent, or the engine is dirty, the worst that can occur is the stoppage of the engine and loss of time.

Fire Insurance Companies charge no extra premium when petroleum engines are used in buildings, unless a naked flame is used.

In "relative convenience," in working, petroleum engines appear to have great advantages over steam-engines; while as regards erection, the absence of the boiler and other appliances must be a distinct advantage, especially when large engines are to be used.

PLANT TO BE PROVIDED FOR

	A STEAM-ENGINE.	A GAS-ENGINE.	A PETROLEUM ENGINE.
1.	Furnace to burn coal or wood.	Furnace for coal.	Small oil-tank for storage.
2.	A boiler.	Apparatus for generating gas.	Apparatus for delivery and ignition of oil and air.
3.	A constant water-supply.	Apparatus for cooling and purifying.	Engine cylinder and piston to produce motion.
4.	Apparatus to control delivery of steam.	Gasometer for storage.	Small water-tank to cool cylinder.
5.	An engine cylinder and piston, to produce motion.	Apparatus for delivery and ignition of gas.	Apparatus to control and transmit motion obtained from piston.
6.	Apparatus to control motion obtained from piston.	Engine cylinder and piston to produce motion.	
7.	Condensing apparatus. (in large engines)	Small water-tank to cool cylinder.	
8.	Heat economizers. (in large engines)	Apparatus to control and transmit motion derived from piston.	
9.	Mechanical stokers. (in large engines)		

This table shows at a glance the relative convenience in erection of petroleum engines, but in towns where there is a public supply of gas, the gas-engine is the most convenient for small power-users, because the first four items under the heading "gas-engine" are provided by municipal or private enterprise, while, *if the supply is constant*, the power-user has only to turn a tap and strike a match to start his engine. But in country places, in villages or localities where gas is dear or dirty, gas-engines will find no place.

Steam-engines must be constantly fed with fuel and water, and the smaller they are, the more often they require attention when at full work ; whereas a petroleum engine at full work may be arranged to run for days, or even weeks, with no more attention than is necessary to lubricate the bearings, and in some cases the cylinders.

Again, a steam-engine requires a trained attendant, whereas it is an undoubted fact that any servant of ordinary intelligence can learn in a day or two to work a petroleum engine, at all events up to a certain size, and not only to start or stop it, but also to find out what is wrong, and do the necessary cleaning or replacing of parts.

In both petroleum and steam-engines the fuel must be stored and carried to the engine. Certainly petroleum is handier and cleaner than coal, though its peculiar odour is not liked by most people. In storage it has a decided advantage, inasmuch as one ton of oil and one ton of coal each require about 40 cubic feet of store room, but one ton of oil will do three or four times the work of one ton of coal.

Relative economy.—This is a most difficult point to treat briefly, as so many factors have to be considered. The main expense in a petroleum engine is the fuel itself. At the present moment Russolene petroleum costs under 3*d*. per gallon *ex quay* English ports.

A gallon of Russolene weighs on an average 8¼ lbs., therefore 1 cwt. equals say 13½ gallons, which at 3*d*. per gallon equals 3*s*. 4½*d*. per cwt. Therefore 3*s*. 4½*d*. plus cost of delivery is the basis on which each power-user can base his calculations for comparison with other engines.

I may here again point out that there is no waste in handling this fuel, provided that the receptacles are well made.

The price of the fuel is thus easily arrived at, but the commercial power-user requires also a guide as to the useful effect he will get from this expensive fuel. He will naturally turn to the catalogues of manufacturers.

As a rule, however, engine-makers' catalogues are compiled more for the technical than the commercial public. Some reckon by nominal horse-power, some by indicated horse-power, some by brake horse-power, and some by effective horse-power.

The term "nominal horse-power" is purely nominal, and it is not easy to see why it should ever be used in connection with oil-engines, unless to puzzle buyers.

The indicated horse-power is the sum of the interior and exterior work (see page 62), which is the true measure of the total energy exerted in the cylinder on the piston; while the brake or effective horse-power is, or should be, the measure of the power available for transmission to any given duty.

The ratio between the effective horse-power and the indicated horse-power is called the *mechanical efficiency* of the engine.

Again, every fuel gives out a certain amount of energy or heat while burning. The amount of that heat or energy which is eventually utilized on the piston of the engine may be called the *fuel efficiency*.

A little reflection will show that the interior work of any engine must depend not only upon the details of

construction and general design, but also upon the amount
of friction, which is a factor varying from day to day, and
dependent on circumstances, such as speed, lubrication,
cleanliness, etc., and which can only be gauged by actual
experiment at a given time. It is quite a common experience that small steam-engines which may give an
effective horse-power for 4 lbs. of coal on a fair trial in the
maker's shop, will be found to require 8 lbs. after twelve
months' work in ignorant or careless hands. The fuel
efficiency has decreased through deposits on the heating
surfaces, and the mechanical efficiency has decreased owing
to increased friction.

Petroleum engines are not so liable to this form of
deception, because they are self-stoking, and may be self-
lubricating, while any dirt or deposit stops the engine, and
thereby calls attention very forcibly to the faults of the
attendant.

Nevertheless, some attention must be given, and no
maker can *guarantee* a continued effect from a cwt. of oil
unless the engine is under his care, and he supplies the
oil, but the effect which the buyer may fairly expect from
an engine can be arrived at in another way; that is, the
maker can guarantee the indicated horse-power when a
certain kind of oil is used, or in other words he can
guarantee the fuel-efficiency.

If the purchaser has some information on the constituents and heating power of various oils, he can analyze
the oil he intends to use, and form his own judgment as
to whether a given engine will suit his wants.

Thus, if a power-user asks the question, "What effect

can I expect from a cwt. of Russolene oil in a petroleum engine?" he must make some such calculation as this to obtain an answer.

One pound of Russolene oil will yield when exploded say 19,000 heat-units. Of this say 60 per cent. will escape through the cylinder, and say 25 per cent. through the exhaust and chimney, leaving 15 per cent. as work done in the cylinder on the piston, that is, 2850 (15 per cent. of 19,000) heat-units have yielded up their energy in moving the piston forward. Of these 2850, about one-fifth may be assumed to be used in the interior work of the engine, leaving 2280 heat-units available for exterior, useful work.

It is hardly necessary now-a-days to point out that heat and power are transposable terms.

One heat-unit is 772 foot-pounds.

One horse-power is 33,000 foot-pounds per minute.

Therefore one horse-power hour is 1,980,000 foot-pounds; therefore if one pound of oil yields (2850 × 772) 2,200,200 foot-pounds, one cwt. will yield (2,200,200 × 112) 246,400,000 foot-pounds, which divided by 1,980,000 gives 124 horse-power hours, and therefore one cwt. of oil, value 3s. 4½d. plus cost of delivery, should keep a petroleum engine at useful work for 124 horse-power hours.

I have made this calculation at length, because any fuel may be treated in the same way, if its heat value is known. Thus, one pound of Scotch shale lamp-oil is estimated to contain 19,700 heat-units, while one pound of average coal contains about 14,000 heat-units. To present a comparison of the effect of the universal fuel coal, with the above figures—

Take one cwt. of coal, value say 9*d.*, one pound of which will yield, when burned, 14,000 heat-units. Coal cannot be burned like oil in the engine cylinder; its heat has to pass from a furnace, through metal, to water, transform the water to steam, and in that form it arrives in the cylinder. In these transformations 13,300 heat-units will probably disappear. The exact amount lost will depend on the design of boiler and engine, but in the best designs 12,500 will be lost.

Assuming, however, 700 heat-units to survive and be converted into work in the cylinder by motion of the piston, one-seventh will be required for the interior work of the engine, and 600 remain for useful work from one pound of coal, as against 2280 from one pound of Russolene oil. By calculation as before, one cwt. of coal would yield 30 horse-power hours.

The above calculations are only to be taken as examples of average results deduced from experience. In a small cheap steam boiler and engine not half the above result might be obtained.

Some relative efficiencies of different heat-engines are given by Sir Guildford Molesworth, the well-known engineer (see Appendix A, Table I.).

This table is a very useful one in giving the relative values of various heat-engines, viz. steam, and gas, and hot-air, which all use coal as primary source of heat, and it includes one engine which uses petroleum explosively. In compiling this table such an authority as Sir G. Moles-

worth may fairly be assumed to be correct in the relative
values, even though absolute values might be disputed.
It will be seen that with the exception of large steam-
engines which have all the best fuel and heat-saving
apparatus, the petroleum engine has a far greater fuel-
efficiency than any of the others.

It is highly probable that the fuel-efficiency will be
increased by further improvements, and should the fuel
cost decrease by even one-third, the petroleum engine
will take the highest rank in "relative economy" of fuel,
although the mechanical efficiency must always be less
than that of the steam-engine, as there is more internal
work to be done.

In the last competitive trials held by the Royal Agricul-
tural Society, the first prize was adjudged to a petroleum
engine the mechanical efficiency of which was 0·83. This
engine was selected as the best all-round engine for farm-
yard work, but there were others which showed a still
higher efficiency. One engine reached the very satisfactory
figure of 0·88, and consumed only 0·73 lb. of Russolene
oil per horse-power per hour. In the portable engine trials
the winning engine used only eighty gallons of water in
a three days' run of twenty-two hours.

The following table may be of assistance to power-
users.

SKETCH of annual working cost of an engine of 5 effective horse-power, working for 10 hours per diem for 300 working days per annum.

STEAM-ENGINE.	Rate.	£	s.	COAL-GAS ENGINE.	Rate.	£	s.	PETROLEUM ENGINE.	Rate.	£	s.
Coal for 15,000 h.p. hours, allow 1 ton for 400 h.p. hours + 10% for waste in handling and getting up steam.				Gas for 15,000 h.p. hours, allow 3000 cub. ft. for 100 B. h.p. hours [1]............				Oil for 15,000 h.p. hours, allow 1 cwt. per 100 h.p. hours...			
								Oil for starting and ignition, 1 gal. per diem			
Lubricants, allow 3 lbs. per 100 h.p. hours ...				Lubricants, allow 3 lbs. per 100 h.p. hours...				Lubricants, allow 3 lbs. per 100 B. h.p. hours			
Stores and material ...				Stores and material ...				Stores and material ...			
Wages for driving, cleaning, repairing, allow 1¼ men per diem				Wages for driving, cleaning, repairing, allow ⅓ man per diem				Wages for driving, cleaning, repairing, allow ¼ man per diem			
Interest on capital				Interest on capital				Interest on capital			
Depreciation fund, allow 10 years' life............				Depreciation fund, allow 15 years' life				Depreciation fund, allow 15 years' life			
Raising water 250 tons...				Water to raise 25 tons				Water to raise 25 tons			
Removing dirt, ashes, etc. 6 tons.............								For electric ignition add 2d. per diem ...			

[1] Late improvements in gas-engines claim to reduce this amount by one-third.

No estimate of cost is shown in the preceding table, because of the ever-varying prices of material in different countries. Every power-user knows the prices in his own district, and can fill up the estimates and make his own comparisons. If he lives in a town where gas is sold at a reasonable price, he will prefer a gas-engine; if he lives in a country where wood and water are easily obtained, he will prefer a steam-engine; but there are thousands of places where there is no gas available, and where no steam-engine is even possible. There is the field for the petroleum engine at present; always provided that the cost of petroleum is not excessive. And it cannot be too much emphasized that in all parts of the world petroleum might be a cheap and plentiful fuel if import dues were abolished. Storage on a large scale at sea-ports is absolutely necessary for a cheap and constant inland supply, while cheap freights must be by tank steamer and special appliances.

Unless foreign governments will put petroleum fuel, as regards duty, on the same footing as coal fuel, capital will not be forthcoming for those purposes. At present coal is very properly admitted at low tariffs as being a necessity of existence, while petroleum appears to be regarded as a luxury to be highly taxed. If, however, petroleum is found to be a cheaper and more effective fuel than coal, it is hoped that these governments will re-consider the tariffs, and admit petroleum free or at very low duties. Then the future of the petroleum engine will begin.

CHAPTER XI

IT would be very difficult at present to foretell the future development of this valuable natural product. It has already become the most generally useful illuminant of the day, and in this respect it will probably increase in popularity. It fully realizes the demand for a cheap and good light, and is independent of the costly installations required for gas or electricity. When petroleum was first obtained in large quantities, the only, or almost the only, use it was put to was for the preparation of lighting oils. The bye products, however, soon found a demand, and lubricating oils, medical preparations, and paraffin wax were manufactured. These were followed in Russia by the application of the heavy residue remaining after the lighter products had been distilled over to heating, and this "liquid fuel" soon became greatly used on the South Russian railways and Caspian Sea steamers. In the United States a fresh field for some of the heavier distillates was found in the enrichment of gas. This application has been recently introduced into Great Britain, and has met with considerable success. In this direction it may be anticipated that a much larger demand will follow on the first successful introduction. Perhaps the most marked success in new adoptions of petroleum to practical purposes is found in the motors generally known as "petroleum engines," which but a very few years since were looked on as toys by practical engineers, and which have now become rivals to the steam-engine. These engines are capable of being adopted for many varied purposes, among others that of replacing the various methods of transmission of power, because a petroleum engine can be used in the most inaccessible places, where if necessary the supply of oil can be conveyed through a pipe.

Another direction in which great advance has been made of late is in the construction of stoves for domestic and industrial use. Whatever novel applications may be within the possible range of invention, the increase in the consumption of petroleum will lie in the further development of appliances for the production of light, heat, and power in this country, provided we can obtain a sufficient supply at a moderate cost. The reserves of petroleum must not be considered as inexhaustible, but we have sufficient evidence to prove that immense quantities of crude oil are to be found in many parts of the world, and with the present improved mode of transport, these supplies can be, and no doubt will some day be made available and brought to this market. The increased demand for petroleum in this country is the more certain to take place as it enters free of duty. In most other countries a heavy duty is imposed on refined, and a light one on crude oil. The result of this system is to protect the trade of refining within the limits of the territory. There is no reason why crude oil should not be imported into the United Kingdom, and the process of refining carried out here as elsewhere. In fact it appears strange that this has never been carried out.

The process, as already briefly described, consists in the fractional distillation of the crude oil, by means of which it is subdivided into a number of distillates, according to the temperature at which they pass from the still, thus producing a variety of oils varying in density, flashing point, and colour, and known by a corresponding difference in designation. The different grades or divisions are arbitrarily adopted by manufacturers to suit the kind of crude oil treated, and the special requirements of the market to be supplied. Hence in countries where crude oil is imported and locally refined, it is divided into such products as suit the needs of the public. This is clearly in favour of local treatment. The future development of the petroleum trade in this country depends primarily on a good supply at moderate cost, and it appears to me that the best way to insure this is to import crude oil from points where it exists, and which lie within easy transport of this country. The sources from which it might be derived would be, for example, the West India Islands and the South American Atlantic coast. Petroleum is known to exist in Mexico, Venezuela, and Argentina, but has not yet been raised in any quantity in these countries, nor would there be much inducement to do so if the object was confined to supplying these countries with kerosene. But if we take into consideration the broader view of the question, namely, that of supplying Europe with crude oil, an immense market would at once be available.

There are many other parts of the world besides those just enumerated where petroleum has been proved to exist, and which might eventually be brought to the home market. Prominent among these we must place the large fields of North-west Canada, which are waiting for some means of communication with the sea-board; and among recent developments, mention must also be made of those which have taken place in the far East, in Java, Sumatra, Borneo, etc., which promise good results. Possibly a future supply to this country might be obtained from these far-off fields in spite of the great distance, which can be overcome by means of the comparatively cheap transport by tank-steamers.

The future of petroleum in this country depends in a great measure on development in this direction. It is needless to point out that our present supply is derived from two sources only, namely, the United States and Russia, and any alteration in the existing circumstances of the trade would indubitably lead to a rise in the price, which, although probably not affecting the use of the illuminating oils, would greatly impede an extended consumption of petroleum for industrial purposes.

APPENDIX A

TABLE I.

(SIR G. MOLESWORTH.)

Shows the percentage of theoretical heat or combustion which is rendered into useful work by different motors.

	Per cent.
By small high-pressure engine without expansion	1·8
„ Ericson's hot-air engine	1·8
„ Lehman's hot-air engine	1·8
„ Lenoir's gas-engine	2·0
„ portable steam-engine	2·8
„ high-pressure steam-engine with expansion	3·0
„ hot-air engine (Leavitt's)	3·5
„ „ · „ (Belou's)	4·1
„ condensing engine with expansion	4·5
„ gas-engine (Otto & Langen)	5·0
„ petroleum engine	8·4
„ large steam-engine, best make	9·0

Flashing point of mineral oils which may be legally used as lamp oils in various countries.

United Kingdom	73° Fahr. (close test).
Russia	82° ,,
America	100° ,, (open test).
France	100° ,, (open test).
Germany	70° ,, (close test).
Switzerland	95° ,, (open test).
Austria	100° ,, (open test).
India	110° ,, (close test).

TABLE II.

(MOLESWORTH AND UNWIN.)

Shows relative heats of perfect combustion of one pound of various fuels.

Average coal being 1·00—

Wood	is	0·58
Scotch shale oil (1st run)	„	0·80
Steam coal	„	1·15
Patent fuel briquettes ...	„	1·18
Anthracite coal	„	1·20
Russolene lamp oil ...	„	1·35
Royal Daylight lamp oil	„	1·40
Scottish shale lamp oil ...	„	1·42

USEFUL MEMORANDA.

1 Imperial gallon water weighs 10 lbs.
1 Imperial gallon lamp oil, average weight, 8¼ lbs.
1 American gallon lamp oil, average weight, 7 lbs.
6 American gallons equal 5 Imperial gallons.
1 horse-power hour is equal to 1,980,000 foot-pounds.
1 horse-power hour equals 2570 heat-units.
1 kilogramme = 2·2 lbs.
1 hectolitre = 22 Imp. gallons.
1 pood (Russian) = 36 lbs. = 3·6 Imp. gallons (water)
1 Oke (Egyptian) = 2·7 lbs.
1 Chô (Japan) = 1·6 quarts.
1 Imp. gallon = 4·537 litres.
1 U.S. gallon = 3·80 litres.
1 U.S. barrel = 35 Imp. gallons = 42 U.S. gallons.

G

APPENDIX B

London County Council.

PUBLIC CONTROL DEPARTMENT,

21, WHITEHALL PLACE, S.W.

July 1893.

PETROLEUM LAMPS.

In view of the numerous fatal and other accidents caused by Petroleum Lamps, the Council considers it desirable to make public the following suggestions, which are partly founded on recommendations made by SIR FREDERICK ABEL, C.B., D.C.L., F.R.S., *and* MR. BOVERTON REDWOOD, F.I.C., F.C.S., *after investigating the causes of lamp accidents.*

Suggestions as to the Construction and Management of Petroleum (or Paraffin) Lamps.

CONSTRUCTION OF LAMPS.

1.—The wick should be enclosed in a tube of thin sheet metal, open at the bottom. This wick tube should reach almost to the bottom of the reservoir containing the oil.

2.—The oil reservoir should be of metal, and not of china, glass, or other fragile material.

3.—The upper part of the lamp which comprises the burner, wick-tube, etc., should be constructed to securely screw into the metal reservoir.

4.—The oil reservoir should have no feeding-place nor opening other than the opening into which the upper part of the lamp is screwed.

5.—Every lamp should have a broad and heavy base, and a proper extinguishing apparatus.

WICKS.

6.—Wicks should be soft, and not tightly plaited, and should quite fill the wick-holder without having to be squeezed into it.

7.—Wicks should be dried at the fire before being put into lamps, and should be soaked with oil before being lit.

MANAGEMENT.

8.—The reservoir should be **quite filled with oil every time** before using the lamp.

9.—The lamp should be kept thoroughly clean, all oil should be carefully wiped off, and all charred wick and dirt removed before lighting.

10.—When first lit, the wick should be partially turned down, and then slowly raised.

11.—Lamps which have no extinguishing apparatus should be put out as follows :—The wick should be turned down until there is only a small flickering flame, and a sharp puff of breath should be sent **across** the top of the chimney, **but not down it.**

12.—Cans or bottles used for oil should be free from water and dirt, and should be kept thoroughly closed.

ALFRED SPENCER,
Chief Officer.

NOTE.—These suggestions apply to ordinary **Petroleum** or **Paraffin** lamps such as are generally used, and not to **Benzoline** or **Spirit** lamps.

.APPENDIX C

CALORIFIC VALUE OF CRUDE OIL ACCORDING TO DR. GINTL.

	FRENCH CALORIES.	BRITISH HEAT UNITS.
West Virginia	10,180	18,324
Pennsylvania	9,963	17,933
Java	10,831	19,495
Baku	11,460	20,628
East Galicia	10,085	18,153
West Galicia	10,231	18,415
Roumania	10,005	18,009
Methane	13,065	23,517
Ethylene	11,850	21,330

APPENDIX D

IMPORT DUTIES ON CRUDE AND REFINED PETROLEUM IN DIFFERENT COUNTRIES.

(Given approximately in English money and cwts.)
(1 cwt. = 14 gallons.)

	CRUDE.	REFINED.
Austria	2s.	10s.
France	7s. 2d.	12s. 6d.
Germany	3s.	3s.
Holland	5½d.	5½d.
Italy	12s. 6d.	15s. 6d.
Portugal	5d.	14s.
Spain	12s. 6d.	16s.

BRITISH COLONIES.

Canada	Kerosene	... ...	3½d. per gallon.
Cape of Good Hope	,,	... ...	6d. ,,
India	,,	... ...	free ,,
Newfoundland ...	,,	... ...	3d. ,,
New South Wales	,,	... ...	6d. ,,
New Zealand ...	,,	... ...	6d. ,,
South Australia	,,	... ...	3d. ,,
Queensland ...	,,	... ...	6d. ,,
Tasmania ...	,,	... ...	6d. ,,
Victoria	,,	... ...	6d. ,,
West Australia ...	,,	... ...	4½d. ,,

www.ingramcontent.com/pod-product-compliance
Lightning Source LLC
Chambersburg PA
CBHW021414090426
42742CB00009B/1136